SIMPLY SCIENCE

# Rocks

## by Alice K. Flanagan

Content Adviser: Terrence E. Young Jr., M.Ed., M.L.S.,
Jefferson Parish (La.) Public Schools

Reading Adviser: Dr. Linda D. Labbo,
Department of Reading Education, College of Education,
The University of Georgia

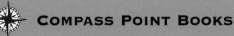

COMPASS POINT BOOKS

Minneapolis, Minnesota

Compass Point Books
3722 West 50th Street, #115
Minneapolis, MN 55410

Visit Compass Point Books on the Internet at *www.compasspointbooks.com* or e-mail your
request to *custserv@compasspointbooks.com*

Photographs ©:

Muskovac Enterprises/Colephoto, cover; Root Resources/Louise K. Broman, 4; Visuals Unlimited/A.J. Copley, 5; Photo Network/
Grace Davies, 6; Root Resources/John Kohout, 7 top; Visuals Unlimited/A.J. Copley, 7 bottom; Visuals Unlimited/Kevin and
Betty Collins, 8; Visuals Unlimited/D. Cavagnaro, 9; Joseph Bailey/Colephoto, 10; Unicorn Stock Photos/Frank Pennington,
11 left; James P. Rowan, 11 middle; International Stock/Warren Faidley, 11 right; Joe Bailey/Colephoto, 12; Sharon Gerig/Tom
Stack and Associates, 13 left; Visuals Unlimited/Ken Lucas, 13 middle, 13 right; Richard Hamilton Smith, 14; Unicorn Stock
Photos/Lee M. Watson, 15; Robert Fried/Tom Stack and Associates, 16; Index Stock Imagery, 17; John Shaw/Tom Stack and
Associates, 18; Index Stock Imagery/Keren Su, 19; Visuals Unlimited/M. Long, 20; Brian Parker/Tom Stack and Associates, 22;
Visuals Unlimited/Martin G. Miller, 23; Visuals Unlimited/D. Cavagnaro, 24; James P. Rowan, 25; Mark Newman/Tom Stack and
Associates, 27; Marilyn Moseley LaMantia, 28.

Editors: E. Russell Primm, Emily J. Dolbear, and Melissa Stewart
Photo Researcher: Svetlana Zhurkina
Photo Selector: Dawn Friedman
Design: Bradfordesign, Inc.

**Library of Congress Cataloging-in-Publication Data**

Flanagan, Alice K.
    Rocks / by Alice K. Flanagan.
        p. cm.—(Simply science)
    Includes bibliographical references (p.    ) and index.
    Summary: A brief introduction to the type of rocks on earth and how
    they are formed.
    ISBN 0-7565-0033-8 (hardcover : lib. bdg.)
        1. Rock—Juvenile literature. [1. Rocks.]   I. Title.
        II. Simply science (Minneapolis, Minn.)
    QE432.2.F55 2000
    552—dc21                                                      00-008558

# Table of Contents

# What's a Rock Made Of?

Pick up a rock. How does it feel? What shape and color is it? These things will tell you what kind of a rock it is.

Rocks are made of **minerals**. Each mineral looks different. Some are green, and some are gray. Some are brown, and some are white. Some are shiny, and some are dull. Some are hard, and some are soft. There are hundreds of different kinds of minerals.

*Rocks can be many different colors and sizes.*

*Quartz is a mineral that comes in different colors.*

## Earth's Crust

Rocks are everywhere. No matter 2
where you go, you can see them. Look
for them along the edge of the road,
in a forest, or in a field. There are also
rocks on the bottom of the ocean and
on the top of a mountain.
If you dig into the
ground, you will
find more rocks.
Soil is a mixture
of broken-up
rocks and bits
of dead plants
and animals.

*The inside of a rock can be very beautiful.*

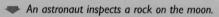

Sand is made of tiny pieces of rock.

An astronaut inspects a rock on the moon.

The layer of rock that makes up Earth's surface is called the crust. **Earth's crust** covers the world the way a piecrust covers an apple pie. Most of Earth's crust is made of a kind of rock called **igneous rock**.

# Igneous Rock

The word *igneous* means "made from fire." **Igneous rock** is made when hot melted rock cools down. Deep inside Earth, it is very hot. All that heat can melt underground rock. The melted rock is called **magma**. Sometimes magma pushes up, or **erupts**, through an opening in Earth's crust. Then we call the melted rock **lava**.

The Grand Teton mountains

Lava flowing

When lava cools, it becomes very hard.
We call it igneous rock. 6

Sometimes lava builds up in piles
around an opening in the Earth's crust.
Over time, the piles make a mountain
called a volcano.

▲ Mount Saint Helens after its eruption

New lava flow on old soil

Lava rock in Iceland

A volcano erupting in Hawaii

There are about 500 active volcanoes in the world today that could erupt. The most famous volcano in the United States is Mount Saint Helens in the state of Washington.

Granite is one kind of igneous rock. It was once magma. Granite can be white, gray, pink, or red. Sometimes granite is a mix of many different colors.

Many mountains are made of granite. Mount Rushmore is a famous granite mountain in South Dakota.

Basalt is another kind of igneous rock. It can be brown, green, red, or black. Diamonds are the hardest igneous rocks in the world. Talc is the softest.

*Basalt columns*

*Talc*

*Rough diamond*

*Mount Rushmore honors four American presidents.*

# Sedimentary Rock

Some rocks are made of tiny pieces of shells, sand, mud, and pebbles. Wind and water carry these materials, called sediment, to lakes and oceans. The sediment falls to the ocean floor and forms a layer there.

As time passes, the layers of sediment pile up. The layers on top press down on the layers below. Slowly, the bottom layers turn into rock. It takes millions of years to make **sedimentary rock**.

Layers of sandstone and siltstone in sedimentary rock

A river carries sediment to the ocean.

You can see many layers of this colorful sedimentary rock at the Grand Canyon in Arizona. A long time ago, the canyon was under water.

Sometimes you can find the outline of an animal or a leaf in sedimentary rock. Such an outline is called a **fossil**.

Sandstone is a kind of sedimentary rock made from sand. Sandstone can be yellow, brown, red, gray, or green.

Limestone is another kind of sedimentary rock. It is made of the shells of tiny ocean animals that lived millions of years ago.

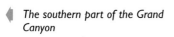
The southern part of the Grand Canyon

A fossil of a fish in sandstone ▶

Some people use limestone to make cement. Then they mix the cement with sand, gravel, and water to make concrete for sidewalks. Other things are made from limestone too. Thousands of years ago, the people of Egypt built giant pyramids out of limestone. You can still see the pyramids today.

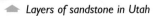

Layers of sandstone in Utah

Pools made of natural limestone in China

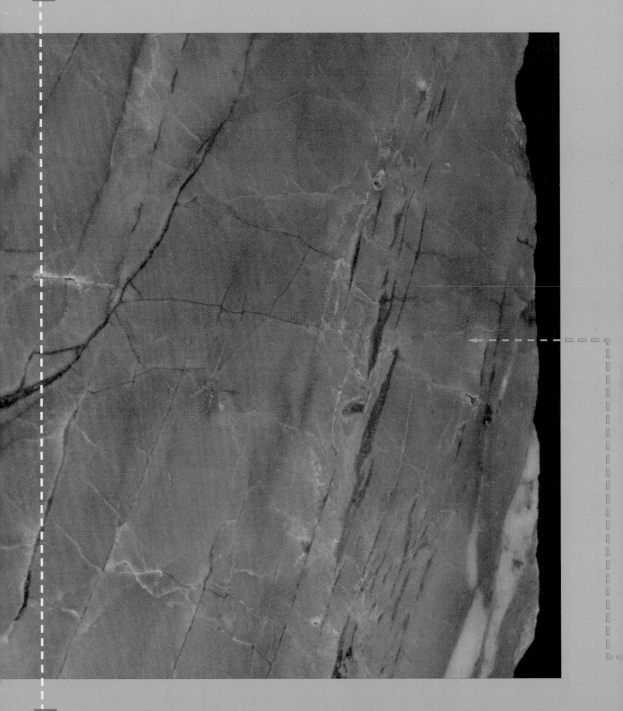

# Metamorphic Rock

Igneous and sedimentary rocks can be changed into **metamorphic rock**. Marble is one kind of metamorphic rock. Marble started out as limestone, which is a kind of sedimentary rock. It takes millions of years for limestone to change into marble.

Pure marble is white. But marble can also be yellow, pink, red, green, gray, or black. The Lincoln Memorial in Washington, D.C., is made of dazzling white marble.

*Pink marble*

◀ The white marble statue of Abraham Lincoln inside the Lincoln Memorial

**Gneiss** (say *nys*) is another kind of metamorphic rock. It started out as granite, which is a kind of igneous rock.

Two things are needed before metamorphic rock can form—heat and pressure. The heat comes from deep inside Earth or from magma and hot gases. The pressure comes from tons of rock pressing down. After many years of heat and pressure, limestone turns into marble and granite turns into gneiss.

*Gneiss*

## Wind and Water

Rocks are changing all the time. Wind and water break them up and wear them away. Wind smashes into rocks and wears away their edges. Pouring rain, crashing waves, and rushing streams hit against rocks and break them into tiny pieces. Snow and ice break up rock too.

*Waves wear down rocks at the shore.*

*Wind created unusual rock sculptures in Utah's Goblin Valley State Park.*

As time passes, rocks are rounded into pebbles that turn into grains of sand. Then they are carried far away by strong winds or rushing rivers. This process, called **erosion**, changes the shape of the land.

*Sandstone erosion in Colorado* ▶

Transit to: PTREE
Transit library: NWEST
Title: Rocks
Item ID: R0095083946
Transit reason: LIBRARY
Transit date: 2/25/2021,16:
03

## Let's Collect Rocks!

Rocks are the oldest things in the world. Many rocks have beautiful colors and shapes. If you go rock

collecting, bring a pen, a small note-book, some masking tape, and a bag. After you choose a rock, write down where you found it. Did you find it on a farm, on a beach, on a mountain, in a desert, or in a city park?

Place a number next to what you wrote. Write the same number on a small piece of masking tape and stick the tape to the rock. Put the rock in your bag, and look for more interesting rocks. Get a book about rocks and minerals from the library to learn about the rocks you found.

*Children organizing their rock collections*

## Glossary

**Earth's crust**—the top layer of Earth

**erosion**—the breaking up or wearing away of rock

**erupts**—pushes up

**fossil**—the remains of a plant or animal that lived long ago

**gneiss**—a common metamorphic rock

**igneous rock**—rock made when hot melted rock cools down

**lava**—melted rock that has pushed up from the inner Earth

**magma**—hot, melted rock beneath Earth's surface

**metamorphic rock**—rock formed by heat and pressure

**minerals**—solid, natural materials of many colors and types. Rocks are made of minerals.

**sedimentary rock**—rock made of shell, sand, mud, and pebbles

## Did You Know?

- Scientists who study rocks are called geologists.

- The jewels in many rings, necklaces, and earrings are minerals.

- If Earth were the size of an orange, the Earth's crust would be about as thick as the orange peel.

# Want to Know More?

## At the Library

Christian, Spencer. *Is There a Dinosaur in Your Backyard?: The World's Most Fascinating Fossils, Rocks, and Minerals.* New York: Wiley, 1998.

Gans, Roma. *Let's Go Rock Collecting.* New York: HarperCollins, 1997.

Morris, Neil. *Rocks & Minerals.* New York: Crabtree, 1998.

Snedden, Robert. *Rocks and Soil.* Austin, Tex.: Raintree Steck-Vaughn, 1999.

## On the Web

**Rock Hounds**

*http://www.fi.edu/fellows/payton/rocks/index2.html*

For information about different types of rocks and rock collecting

**Smithsonian Gem and Mineral Collection**

*http://galaxy.einet.net/images/gems/gems.html*

For pictures and information about many different minerals and gems

## Through the Mail

**U.S. Geological Survey**

USGS National Center

12201 Sunrise Valley Drive

Reston, VA 22092

For maps and advice about good places to collect rocks in your area

## On the Road

**American Museum of Natural History**

Central Park West at 79th Street

New York, NY 10024

212/769-5250

Visit the museum's Hall of Planet Earth, one of the world's best displays of rocks, minerals, and gemstones

# Index

## About the Author

Alice K. Flanagan writes books for children and teachers. Ever since she was a young girl, she has enjoyed writing. She has written more than seventy books on a wide variety of topics. Some of her books include biographies of U.S. presidents and their wives, biographies of people working in our neighborhoods, phonics books for beginning readers, and informational books about birds and Native Americans. Alice K. Flanagan lives in Chicago, Illinois.